DEMETRIA L. BAGNER

Poé Publishing

Unless otherwise noted, Scriptures quoted in this book are from *Holy Bible, Authorized King James Version* Copyright © 1986 by World Bible Publishers,Inc. All Rights Reserved.

Colors of Emotions
All Rights Reserved.
Copyright © 2017 Demetria L. Bagner
v2.0

The opinions expressed in this manuscript are solely the opinions of the author and do not represent the opinions or thoughts of the publisher. The author has represented and warranted full ownership and/or legal right to publish all the materials in this book.

This book may not be reproduced, transmitted, or stored in whole or in part by any means, including graphic, electronic, or mechanical without the express written consent of the publisher except in the case of brief quotations embodied in critical articles and reviews.

Poé Publishing

ISBN: 978-0-578-19109-6

Library of Congress Control Number: 2017938187

Cover Photo © 2017 thinkstockphotos.com. All rights reserved - used with permission.

PRINTED IN THE UNITED STATES OF AMERICA

"AND THE KING SHALL ANSWER AND SAY UNTO THEM, VERILY I SAY UNTO YOU, INASMUCH AS YE HAVE DONE IT UNTO ONE OF THE LEAST OF THESE MY BRETHREN, YE HAVE DONE IT UNTO ME."

HOLY BIBLE, AUTHORIZED KING JAMES VERSION
(MATTHEW 25:40)

Dedication

I dedicate this book to a few of the many special individuals in my life:

To my father and mother who told me to just be myself and encouraged me when I was a child, making me feel as though I could accomplish anything (and I believed you).

To my husband who has been strong enough to stand with me through mild and difficult times, I love you.

To our darling daughters, you are strong and beautiful young ladies who are growing to become strong and beautiful, black women.

Keep up the great work and remember:

Your greatest dreams
Can be accomplished,
Just hold on
While trying to get there;
If your heart is for it,
You can endure it.

                  Love,
                  Mom/Demetria

Acknowledgements

First and foremost, I thank God for blessing me with these creative gifts. Second, I'd like to acknowledge those of you who have encouraged my dreams and ambitions. Thanks to all the late and present great poets (especially Maya Angelou and Amanda Bradley) who have inspired me. Lastly, I thank God again for facilitating the accessibility of a wealth of information through the internet.

Contents

No One Like Me	1
I Still Cry	2
I'm Sorry	3
Playing Games	4
Keeping Up	5
Anything Achievable	6
Acceptance	7
Schedule	8
Slow Down Enough (I)	9
Slow Down Enough (II)	10
And I Appreciate	11
Crimson Worshipper	12
Where Did He Go	13
Depth of Mortality	14
The Moment In Between the Crying	15
My Father Didn't Know	16
Fear	17
Doctor's Visit	18
How the Sun Does	19
Guarded	20
When You Hurt	21
You're Not Alone	23
If I Say . . .	24
Love's Place	25
If God Gave You Back	27
Just Remember	28

No One Like Me

So many different versions to enjoy:
Music,
Videos,
Crafts,
Poetry,
Books,
Paintings,
Drawings,
All types of art . . .
There is an infinite number
Of ways to create it.
No one can create exactly as I do –
No one:
Sees it through these eyes;
Hears it from these ears;
Speaks it from these lips;
Births it through this soul;
Feels it through this heart;
Reviews it with this mind.

I Still Cry

Out of nowhere I cry,
I cry not because you went to heaven
But because you left from here.
I can't see you, talk to you, touch you
And for that I can't believe;
Can't believe you're gone –
Gone forever, it's true
And until the day I see you again,
I'll cry . . .
I'll always cry for you.

I'm Sorry

I allow everyone else to be themselves,
To be their strengths,
Their weaknesses, their flaws;
But to me, I guess you're not supposed to have them –
At least not to the extent that you do . . .
I get irritated, frustrated, angry
When I see these traits in you.
People are very interesting,
I allow them to be who they be;
Why can't I allow you to be yourself
As I strive every day to be me?
I realize now, that I've not been fair
Not to allow you to do your thing;
I love you much with all my heart
Now release me from your wing.
You've been there for me all of my life,
Provided strength and support;
The same patience and kindness I give to others
I should give to you more.
I'm sorry, Mom.

Playing Games

Love,
Family,
Work,
Government,
Money,
LIFE.
Each game has its own set of rules.
Used to maintain order,
The rules within one
Can teach us a lot about
The rules within another –
Learn how to play.

Keeping Up

Going to and fro',
Carrying on with
Our daily on-doings –

Why are we so busy?
Busy keeping up
With other people,
Other businesses,
Other countries.

Can we slow down?
Is it too late?

Anything Achievable

With you
I can achieve anything
And be happy

Without you
I can achieve anything
Yet
Remain void

Acceptance

I gave you the best of me;
I gave you the worst of me;
And yet you love me as I am.
Who, what, where, when, why do I love?
I love you!
I love everything about you.
I love you anywhere,
At all times,
Just because . . .

Schedule

It will take more than a moment to
Embrace sixty minutes;

It will take more than an hour to
Embrace a daily routine;

It will take more than a day to
Embrace a workweek;

It will take more than a week to
Embrace a monthly calendar;

It will take more than a month to
Embrace a fiscal year;

It will take more than a year to
Embrace all of life's little comforts;

It will take more than a lifetime to
Embrace God.

Take time to get organized!

Slow Down Enough (I)

Slowdown
Enough to take a deep breath,
Slowdown
Enough to enjoy the tiny moments.
Slowdown
Enough to listen to the wind,
Slowdown
Enough to enjoy the tiny moments.
Slowdown
Enough to view the moon,
Slowdown
Enough to enjoy the tiny moments.
Slowdown
Enough to smell the soil,
Slowdown
Enough to enjoy the tiny moments.
Slowdown
Enough to kiss the morning rain,
Slowdown
Enough to enjoy the tiny moments.
Slowdown
Enough to feel the sun shine,
Slowdown
Enough.

Slow Down Enough (II)

Slowdown
Enough to enjoy the tiny moments,
Slowdown
Enough to breathe, "I like you."
Slowdown
Enough to enjoy the tiny moments,
Slowdown
Enough to listen to him.
Slowdown
Enough to enjoy the tiny moments,
Slowdown
Enough to look him in the eyes.
Slowdown
Enough to enjoy the tiny moments,
Slowdown
Enough to smell his skin.
Slowdown
Enough to enjoy the tiny moments,
Slowdown
Enough to touch his soul.
Slowdown
Enough to enjoy the tiny moments,
Slowdown
Enough to taste his lips.
Slowdown
Enough.

And I Appreciate

I see everyday people that need
Help
They depend on others for sight
And I appreciate . . .
I appreciate the color of my eyes;
I see every day people that need
Help
They depend on others for balance
And I appreciate . . .
I appreciate a bike ride to the corner store;
I see everyday people that need
Help
They depend on others for strength
And I appreciate . . .
I appreciate the Might that is within me;
I see every day people that need
Help
They depend on others for courage
And I appreciate . . .
I appreciate a good effort any day;
I see everyday people that need
Help
They depend on others for speech
And I appreciate . . .
I appreciate discussions that last for hours;
I see every day people that need
Help
They depend on others for thought
And I appreciate . . .
I appreciate coming to my own conclusion.

Crimson Worshipper

The crimson worshipper is one of many,
She travels to and fro'
Mostly, she's at peace with her surroundings
'Cept when enemies come to invade her;
Check her out, she's pretty,
Basking in her (own) glory!
She knows more than we know about ourselves,
I'm here to tell her story:
She's always young,
She regenerates,
She gives no 'absences' and never 'lates';
Given in kindness, work's not a chore,
Serve her diligently,
Yep, you bet, she'll serve you more!

Where Did He Go

Where did my daddy go?
He was just here
I touched him, I should know.
I can see him, I can feel him,
I know it is he
But he's silent and still, he won't talk to me.
Where could all that chatter have gone?
It just up and went.
Now I find talking to myself
Is how my own days are spent.
Where did my daddy go?
I don't understand,
How God could leave me without this man.
What theory, what mechanism caused him to go?
I don't understand
Does anyone know?
I mean, I know this life is temporary
But what caused him to go?
I really don't understand
Does anybody know?
What takes the breath right out of a man?
What breaks him down and not allow him to stand?
What grabs his spirit and takes it away?
What makes his heart not beat today?
Or ever for that matter, not ever again,
What makes a daughter lose her father, her friend?

Depth of Mortality

When I realized the depth of my mortality,
My death became more scary
And my life became more fun.
I learned to appreciate a single workday
And my mind stopped yearning for the weekend.

Now I live 365 days out of the year
And I am at peace with myself.

I am more full, more fun, more free;
I am more alive, more happy, more me.
I know that the only thing I can really count on
Is my here and now,
For my tomorrow may never be.

The Moment In Between the Crying

Did you ever miss someone so much it hurt?
It hurt in your heart, it hurt in your mind,
It hurt with everything you had inside.
Did you go back and sit at the places they sat?
Did you reminisce inside yourself so much you couldn't help that?
You couldn't help that you cried until the tears were no more,
You couldn't help that you were contemplating either/or;
Either to make yourself busy so you wouldn't feel pain
Or to allow your grievance and weather the rain.
Did you think until you thought that your mind would explode?
Did you cry out to God until He took your load?
Did he settle and calm you at least for a moment?
Did He help you to inventory how your own days were spent?
Did this cause you to cry out to Him and call on Him more
For more understanding and guidance than you possessed before?
And when each moment was through that He gave you calm
Did your mind travel back to that person embalmed?
Then call out again, at least for a time,
The moment grows longer each time that you cry.

My Father Didn't Know

My father didn't know
The pain I'd be in;
I think if he did
He would have never gone.
He would have fought heaven and hell
To stay strong.
He'd be here with me
Even now as I write,
He would add his own lines
And we'd probably fight;
Fight over what to say
And how to bring this across;
To let the world know
That his spirit's not lost.
I smile because I realize
As I cross out and rewrite,
He's letting me know
That we're having that fight!

Fear

Living each day in fear
Will take up you time,
It will consume your energy
And paralyze your mind;
Fear is the absence of power in you being,
Being able to live as you may.
Fear is the lack of control in your thought,
The thought, that you have no control anyway.
To be consumed with fear
Each day and each night
That you look behind yourself
When there's no one in sight,
Just confirms your suspicion
That there's someone around;
It's your friend fear
Taking lead and picking up ground!
He's taking over your mind, body, and soul.
If you want to be free
Don't do as you're told!
Don't listen to him.
Don't do as he says;
You've allowed him to get close,
Now, unmake him your friend!
Rebuke him, cast him down
And stand tall –
'Cause if you're living in fear,
You're not living, at all!

Doctor's Visit

Just because you're afraid to know
And you don't want to go
Doesn't make the truth go away;
So run toward the truth
As fast as you can
No man is an island,
No island a man;
Is this that fear we spoke of
That has you not seek
A doctor's glove?
You won't know in in time
'Til you stand strong;
You don't know where illness
Is trying to belong;
To belong to you
Or some body else
Is a decision that's been made
In spite of yourself!
So run toward the truth
Run as fast as you do –
'Cause what you don't know
Can hurt you!

How the Sun Does

How the sun does dance
As it does dance upon my face;
With such poise and glee,
With such style and grace;
As it reflects its strength
Like an aged wine;
My highlights do radiate
Through its shine.
Its journey's brief,
As it means no harm;
Beads of heat
Dance upon my arm;
I can see its glow,
Though my eyes are closed
Its beauty in this moment, I suppose,
Is enough to set the captive mind free,
Is enough to bring a 'pleasure' smile from me.
It's my way to spend my time alone,
It's my turn to exhale a comfort moan.
How the sun does do such things to me –
I've found fortress, I've found friend,
I've found energy.

Guarded

I always
Have my guard up
'Cept when I'm home with you
If you suddenly become a stranger
I'll ask my guard to
Escort me home
Too

When You Hurt

To hurt your heart
Hurts mine,
When I see sadness
In your eyes.

You're in confusion, hurt, anger,
Not sure
Could be all of these
Could be more.

A feeling of
Emotion encompasses me
Please come and set
Me free.

I love the way
You used to smile,
A frown
Has taken over now.

Sustain my heart
By giving me
A hug, a kiss
Or anything!

I didn't mean to make
You worry,
Or is it you
Don't worry, anyway?

I didn't want to make
You mad,
I like the way
We used to be.

I need some
Reassurance now,
That you'll always
Be loving me.

You're Not Alone

You're not alone, I am with you.
I plan to always be
Right beside you day and night;
You in turn, must allow me
To take your hand and hold it,
Forever and a day
And with our lives we'll be molded
Into one and so I pray:

Dear God,

Please keep us together,
Build a love that will last and that will stay,
Create a bond that must not ever break,
This is what I pray.

You're not alone I'm confirming
Something I thought you knew;
There is comfort in the space between my arms,
A space made just for you.

If I Say…

If I say I love you with everything I have in me,
Does that mean my intestines love you too?
If I say I would move heaven and earth to get to where you are,
Does that mean they won't be in their original locations anymore?
If I say I would do anything to make you happy,
Does that mean I'd even do the unthinkable?
If I say you've made me the happiest person in the world,
Does that mean there's no one happier?
If I say I've found everything I need in you,
Does that mean I have everything I need to survive?
If I say I've been waiting for you all of my life,
Does that mean I've been idle?
If I say I only have eyes for you,
Does that mean I can't see anything else?
If I say there's room in my heart for only you,
Does that mean there's love for no one else?
If I say I will love you forever,
Does that mean through always is my intent?
I think then you should expect nothing less
Than for me to be speaking literally.

Love's Place

I knew the moment you left me you felt my pain.
I screamed so loud I made you feel it.
Beyond the boundaries of these walls
What just happened?

My whole world stopped revolving.
In an instant I lost it all!
And in slow-motion,
I pictured it over and over again.

Why didn't you tell me you were leaving today?
Did you think I'd want to tag along?
We've been together for so long inside this place
I thought we'd be in here forever – this place called love.

Places to go;
Things to do;
You've got people to see.

Why couldn't my love be enough
To hold you in here with me?

Pain,
Agony,
Defeat,

They were all strangers then
And none are welcome now.

But they barged their way in one-by-one.
Now, looking back I can truly say
Our lives together seemed to have brought:
More joy than pain,
More sunshine than rain,
More laughter than tears,
More courage than fears.

Yet, was the depth of our pain that much greater
Than the quality of the joy we felt?

Were the clouds during the rain far darker
Than the level of brightness the sun dealt?

Did the tears cause the tides to rise higher
Than the pitch in our voices as we joked?

Did we plant massive seeds of courage
Only to have tiny weeds of fear cause them to choke?

What happened when you decided
You wanted to share this space with me no longer?
They say what does not kill us will prove to make us stronger.

If God Gave You Back

If God gave you back to me
I would speak to you
As the woman I've become,
Not as that girl I used to be.
I'd speak to you with kindness,
With patience and understanding;
I'd speak to you about my world
And all that it's demanding.

If God gave you back
Even for just a day,
I'd tell you of my troubles
To hear what you had to say.

If God gave you back,
For one day gave you back to me,
We'd sit and talk for hours, dad,
You'd be so proud of me.
I'd somehow find in that time to tell
And somehow make you see
That I finally became the woman
I'd always dreamed to be.

Just Remember

Just remember:
Be strong,
Be ethnic,
Be tall;

Be bright,
Be fair,
Be kind;

Be you,
Be me,
Just be;

Be whatever we want to be . . .
Just remember:

"WHEREFORE GOD ALSO HATH HIGHLY EXALTED HIM, AND GIVEN HIM A NAME WHICH IS ABOVE EVERY NAME: THAT AT THE NAME OF JESUS EVERY KNEE SHOULD BOW, OF THINGS IN HEAVEN, AND THINGS IN EARTH, AND THINGS UNDER THE EARTH; AND THAT EVERY TONGUE SHOULD CONFESS THAT JESUS CHRIST IS LORD, TO THE GLORY OF GOD THE FATHER."

HOLY BIBLE, AUTHORIZED KING JAMES VERSION
(PHILIPPIANS 2:9-11)

www.ingramcontent.com/pod-product-compliance
Lightning Source LLC
Chambersburg PA
CBHW071803040426
42446CB00012B/2688